The Presence of Absence

Poems by

Sandy Coomer

Copyright © 2014 by Sandy Coomer

All rights reserved. No part of this publication may be reproduced, stored in a retrieval system, or transmitted, in any form or by any means, electronic, mechanical, photocopying, recording, or otherwise, except for the inclusion of brief quotations in a review, without prior permission in writing from the author

Cover design: Kristen Wilson

Cover and interior photos: Sandy Coomer

Author photos: Shawn Coomer

ISBN: 978-0-9911915-7-4

Published by Sandy Coomer

Printed in the United States of America

For my father

David Lynn Spencer

who taught me how to find the trail

and how to stay on it

Contents

Part One - Presence

Pilgrimage 9
Waiting for a Tow Truck in the Corner of a Church Parking Lot 10
The Presence of Absence 11
A Ninety-Seven-Year-Old Speaks of Death 12
Cloud Study 13
Definition of a Day 14
Murmurs 15
Mind Reader 16
In Keeping With Trees 17
One Minute After Midnight 18
Early Morning Run 19
When You Write 20
Encounter at a Train Station 21
Summer Storms 22
Mother to Son 23
Surfacing 24
Apples 25
October 26
Ten Minutes of What-If 27
These Words Are for You 28

Part Two - Absence

The "Not" Poem	33
The Taxi	34
Tintern Abbey Revisited	35
The Whistle Blower	36
The Lawyer's Office	37
Bus 64	38
Family Cemetery	39
My Father's Lament	40
Burn After Reading	41
Quiet Me	42
Naming Bones	43
The River	44
Love Like This	45
My 1963	46
How It Started	47
Sister	48
The Cardinal	49
Old Growth Forest	50
The Sugar Maple Speaks	51
Poem for a Cat	52

Part One

Presence

'Cause your presence still lingers here
And it won't leave me alone

Evanescence – "My Immortal"

Pilgrimage

Sometimes she finds herself there.
From her chair in the activities parlor, the board games open,
pieces spilled across the table, sometimes she leans back, looks up,

as if she can see through the white ceiling,
the florescent lights. Sometimes, she closes her eyes, blocks out
the TV, the chatter, the piped music meant to calm, and finds true air

moving to the bottom of her lungs - not the thin,
sterile, conditioned air that primes the threaded carpet bound with lattice edge,
the linoleum hallway, the counters doctored with Kleenex and hand sanitizer.

Sometimes it shifts, becomes the heavy musk
of autumn's rotting leaves, or the mud-slick breath of worms and beetles
churning under a fallen log. Sometimes she tastes full lard in collard greens,

the burn of moonshine stolen from a jar
kept under her father's bed. Then she is nearly there, high to the hip
in plaited tobacco ready for harvest, stretching the shallow hill the tractor will soon slice.

She is there in the little house off the road on a raised plot,
above the gully where the lazy creek gouges the limestone, porous
and brittle as ancient bones. Outside, the pony with corn-silk mane waits, the mutt

with the flash of white at his throat, licks watermelon juice
from the grass. She hears voices, laughter so honest it lifts the wind to her neck,
the first true hint of afternoon storm born in the radiating heat of a stagnant summer.

There, in the secret darkness of an oak grove guarding
the road that climbs Bay Mountain, vestiges of a simple piety reach her and cling,
like burrs and velvet seeds, those things that remain long after she runs through the field.

Waiting for a Tow Truck in the Corner of a Church Parking Lot

I pull to the only shady spot
in the humid August afternoon,
while my car puffs a gray smoke
that smells like roasting metal.
Thin greasy fluids pool and slick
the skillet of asphalt.

The tow truck service promises
help in forty-five minutes;
they call back to add thirty more.
I sweat through my shirt, watch
the cars loyal to their drivers
roll smoothly on the steamy road.

Through the windows
of the student outreach building,
I read verses painted on the wall.
John 3:16. Philippians 4:13.
Psalm 100. I wonder if it's a sin
to pray for an unlocked door,

air-conditioning set high, a kitchen
with cold cokes in the fridge.
*If you think it's hot now, you won't
want to know what Hell feels like,*
says the placard by the road.
I decide to pray for rain.

The Presence of Absence
upon visiting the 9/11 Memorial in New York City

The memorial pools
birth a feeling of sinking, a palpable weight
within the solemn rush of water my eyes
measure as indefinite—for what
is finite in emotion except this ache
of abstraction?

Water roars beneath
names etched through black marble,
the letters hollow, and the lack
of solidity form an essence
I struggle to name. It is concise,
knife-sharp but brittle,

the way loss causes
a certain fragility. This is all I can claim—
this intimate grasp of the invisible,
this drain that echoes life once spoken
with certainty. What I hold now
is a vague passion.

It would be easy
to call it death, but it is not the relentless
ending that haunts me. It is the genesis
of a new reality—heavily alive—
breathing through me this hushed
and beautiful mourning.

A Ninety-Seven-Year-Old Speaks of Death

It will come like wind - stealing
my soul like a candle flame quenched
with a puff of air, the warmth
of my body lifted like a wisp

of smoke from the wick. There will be
rising and it will be disconcerting,
a helium balloon on its way to space.

There will be light, dazzling,
like stars focused in a telescope,
brighter, and then a burst,
a shift like an airplane

equalizing, an impatient urge
to move, to push, to fling earth
far away, a disconnected memory.

There will be silence,
and by listening harder than I
have ever listened, I will know it
as a voice in all the songs of praise.

The light will be a balm across
my face, warm with welcome and full -
color so pure I will see only white.

Cloud Study

veins of stratocumulus, a tributary
stretching a blue-gray valley but not
a river
a feather
from a hawk's tail, the quill straight, strong,
ivory tipped and dipped in dark, but not
a feather
a train
steaming across a bridge, the trestle shuddering
under the burden of what we hoped for -
stay here

this is not a terrifying place so high above the valley
but not a valley, not a feather,
not a train
your face
a prism of space, surrender, catch love's vapor,
before it shifts into something
else

Definition of a Day

- the rain that smears the gray horizon
and the mockingbird that rides on the rim of the squall.

- the cold kitchen I sit in as I wait for the buzz
of my son's alarm clock and his slow shuffle down the stairs.

- the sentence I don't speak because I know he'd rather
hear the wisdom of silence this first day with his new anxiety prescription.

- his slight nod as he slings his backpack over his shoulder,
the surge of his car's engine, the tires splashing through puddles.

- the drone of a quiet house, the lonely purr of warm air
through vents, the dry pages of a poetry book I turn without reading.

- the double jab of my heart – a quick one-two –
when his car returns at dusk and I hear him come in.

Murmurs

They call it phenomenon –
        thousands of starlings swoop and bend
                in a frenzied sky-dance.

They split the column
        of air current and breeze, dip beneath
                the tree line and rise again,

the blue-black wave
        a single entity, not a separation of bodies
                distinct and individual.

They call it murmuration –
        thousands of starlings diving, surging,
                all turning toward the center

with wings wild, riotous.
        Each single bird mimics the others until
                they are not separate, not solo.

They are spirit; they are
        collection; they are anthology of flight.
                They are sweep of skylight.

They call it scale-free correlation –
        an equation that biology can't justify,
                a secret network transformation

as the starlings pulse and pause,
        twist the plane of this dimension to a force
                undisclosed. They are album;

they are symphony. They
        are circuit and unity. They are whisper,
                sigh. They are shout, surprise.

Mind Reader

As a child, I thought I could read my mother's mind.
In the kitchen, when she cut vegetables for supper,
I stood behind her and waited to curl myself into her brain.

The sharp knife thudded against the cutting board.
She swiped a tendril of hair from her face, held the pad
of her palm against her forehead a second too long
and I was in.

The terrifying space through which I tunneled –
high walls and pungent earth – wracked my tiny heart
with woman-sized grief. I buckled under its weight, its holiness
boiling the audacity out of me.

My mother turned, caught my wide stare, and smiled
without saying a word. I knew she closed that door on purpose.

She let me in only as far as either of us could bear.

In Keeping With Trees

for my son

I am learning
how to keep without possessing,
though it goes against my nature
and burns my heart with grief.

My face,
in the window of his leaving,
frets like the broken waters
of the brook tumbling over rocks.

Hold him in your heart,
they say, but my heart isn't
big enough, the jars and drawers
not deep enough to pack him in.

I can't make small
the enormity of life. No one can.
So I listen to trees that are used
to letting go the green in their soul,

that are used to dying
in their winter veil, cradling
spring. There is no easy way
to open. Every birth requires pain,

and every parting,
a lesson on how to love transparently -
holding on like clouds hold the tears
of rivers, like sailors keep the stars.

One Minute After Midnight

All the old men and the young men
Who will die of heart attacks
And in car wrecks are still alive.

They haven't yet climbed out of their warm bed
And into the cocktail of circumstance
That will end what they know about living.

All the girls who will be hit and raped,
The children who will be knifed with cutting words,
Who will start to believe right then and there

That they are less than they thought, all those
Still believe in something, whether they call it
"God" or "Good" or don't call it anything in particular,

But know it as a calm serenity deep inside them.

And what about the mother who will send her babies
To the school down the road? The mind of a killer
Has not yet twisted enough to act on his plan.

And the factory worker, the miner, the salesman,
The postman, none of them has yet heard
The rumor of lay-offs, none of the fathers has yet

Stared into the eyes of a doctor and known, even before
The first word, the diagnosis would be terminal. None
Of the roofers have fallen, none of the bank tellers

Have faced the black muzzle of a gun, none of the dogs
Have been kicked, none of the babies have been shaken,
None of the addicts have taken the last fatal dose.

What kind of day it will be is still open for discussion.

Early Morning Run

It's black when we start, you
thirty minutes up and breakfast
in your stomach, and me,
ten minutes from warm bed.

The darkness, a blanket stitched
with stars, hems us in its woolen
quiet, broken only by our steps
on the trail, our soft rhythm

in concert with the cricket's chant,
the katydid's click, over the palpable
hush that is its own dewy language.
We run as if inside a dream,

passing through the birth of day
as it pinks the sky smooth as slate,
and hums the squirrels, fawns
from their sleepy tumble. Wrens

wrestle the hedgerow as we steal by,
the slow crescendo of light lifting
us from the secret places until we
are solid flesh again, running out

of shadow's embrace. Morning
sweeps golden threads before us,
while the moon in its cloister
tucks the fading stars away.

When You Write

Borrow the words from the apples rotting in the barrel
behind the blue shed,
for they have traveled the path from soil to seedling,
blossom to fruit
and back again. They offer something honest, something warm
in fermenting flesh,
the brown and breathless heart. Or take the words
from the nubby folds
and ridges of hickory bark, or the rounded surface
of an acorn,
or the black husk of a walnut, what's left after a week of rain.
See what you can find
in the butterfly wing carried on the back of three army ants,
or the cone left
after the yellow petals fall from the Black-Eyed Susan,
or the dry grasses
scrambled beside the highway. Or better yet, try the fallen log
with the white lichen
and silken moss, or the stagnant bottom of the river bed,
mud-slick and life-weary.
Surprise yourself at the compost pile, where lingering green
slowly sinks
into a rich black-blown. There is truth in what's left
when color fades
and insight in the bare and perishable beauty
of the earth.
Take the words from the ground up and go from there,
but don't clean them.
Leave the tangles, keep the knots, the smell of the wild dark
promise of death.
Leave the wounds, leave the dirt, so you'll never forget
where you found them.

Encounter at a Train Station

Young man at a train station, two dozen braids
spilling around his shoulders like a modern Medusa,
bedraggled jeans hanging on a too-lean frame,
asks for two dollars, careful not to reach too far.

His eyes do the asking more than his voice,
wide, vagrant eyes, seeing too often the have-nots
mingling with the have-much, but not thinking it unfair,
thinking it the way things are.

He learns which people might have a heart, is still
sometimes surprised. Like the blond lady who says
she has no money, spreading her hands open as if to prove it,
emphasizing with an exaggerated shrug and backward steps

she believes whatever face he puts on might be
contagious. He turns to prove he is no threat, presses
his back against concrete so he can feel something hard
against his bones, something real that won't recede

like the smiles of humanity when he comes close.
Days can be so long, ironing flat the faith he keeps
tucked in, but still ready when a certain light streams
through and something in his soul sings.

Memories last a whole week, and he tries to find one
to live in, searches among the bricks loaded in his head,
and there she is – the blond woman,
a shy smile on her face, one slim hand brushing back curls,

 the other holding a coffee cup she offers as she squats,
shifting her weight to sit beside him, smoothing her skirt.
She has banana bread wrapped in plastic, sticky thick
and slightly warm, but it is her smile right before she leaves

that feeds him, and her hand so light and sweet on his.
He believes he is rich with all the things that matter,
knowing the rest of the day, even as the train doors
slam behind her, he will feel full.

Summer Storms

Stifling was a good word for it –
that summer we waited for the thunder-boomers
to roll across Oklahoma and Arkansas
and spill treasure down on drought-stricken Tennessee.

In our house with no air-conditioning, my mother
watched the soaps and I read books with a wet towel draped
across the back of my neck. Nothing moved
if it didn't have to, not even the flies by the screen door.

A sudden hush made us look up - the shadow
of a low cloud, moving across a bleached-out summer blue.
We waited for a rumble in the west, like a chair
scooting across the wooden floor, but fuller, with promise.

The storms didn't pack much punch, but enough
to hush the heat steaming off our faces, enough to gray the sun
and string out pearls of air. Those minutes the drops
fell, sizzling on the roof, was enough to redeem the day.

Even now, years later, I wait for storms to roll
a fortune of change over me. I stand on the porch, watch
the pregnant clouds burble a pledge of relief
while thunder slaps with authority across my skin.

It brings me back to that summer – the blue-black sky,
the breeze that vowed something new and consuming
within the plans of a stagnant day. I watch the rain fall,
seize the life it brings to a parched and listless soul.

Mother to Son

This is me
        worrying,
recounting what I might have done
        to make you struggle like this.
Was it something I said,
something I forgot to do
those years you counted on me
        to teach you,
to show you?

This is me
        guilty
of imperfection,
of not predicting what you would need
        before you needed it.
I could make excuses
and you would try to understand
or would you.

This is
        me
fearing that my great lapse
was doing what I could do
and still not doing enough
to make you live easy in this world.
All that love and still
        to see you writhe.

I peel back layers
        to find the one undone,
to repair it, replace it
and start again.
Can you and I have a do-over
        now that we know
what could go wrong,
what could hurt like this?

Surfacing

Porpoise
in its mission to sing
the waves down,

shaky legged colt
licked dry, sunflower
peeling back

its coarse seed coat,
field sparrow primping
for a date

with the sky,
butterfly nibbling
the chrysalis, bud

on the sugar maple
pink-tinged, moon
parting clouds,

spores hidden
beneath the fern's fringe,
bubble on water,

tadpole's breath,
salmon leaping toward
home, toward death.

Apples

When Eve saw the fruit, I wonder
if she fathomed the force working against
her slender arm reaching up and up.

I rely on Isaac Newton to straighten things out –
that bump on his head the impetus
to a whole new view of the universe.

What is gravity except that which holds us
to our own, a mystery that works invisible magic,
a careful discipline sealed within the forces

of good for our own good. Look at the planets.
What appeal have they for each other
except that magnetic influence drawn hot

by the solar center? We are always seeking
interface, always stretching just enough
to question, yet not enough to break

our connection to what holds us steady –
that weight, that glory, that God-sense,
the order we both long for and despise.

Eve, with the sweet taste in her mouth,
must have looked up and wondered why
she didn't float away toward heaven's genius.

It is no wonder then, an apple cut on its side
reveals a certain star, a reminder in flesh
that we hover between two worlds.

October

A garden spider wraps
a firefly with sticky silk. His
killing work is quick as he binds
the body in a veil of gray until
it is a lump within the circle
of threads strung by my window.

October brings the writing spiders
and their zig-zag code beneath
yellow and black bodies.
Wolf spiders seek warmth
inside my door; their favorite
fort is a pile of laundry.

I know autumn by its spiders
the same way I know loss
by the fangs that sink beneath
my skin. I can't escape the bite
of death or the way the earth
slowly sinks into winter cold,

unwinding the brilliance
of a life strung in abundance.
The firefly had its summer
of romance and I have had
five decades of light. Perhaps
both of us must accept the dark.

The spider catches a gnat,
hardly a snack, yet he assigns
death to it. He is not such
an ugly thing, this spider who
teaches me life's fragile pose
between living and the dead.

Ten Minutes of What-If

The paper gown rustles with every move.
Even when I brush back a wayward strand
of hair, I hear it crinkle like the dry exoskeleton
a cicada leaves on the trunks of trees.

I hold it closed across my chest like I am
protecting myself from something. In the little
curtained room outside the bigger room
with the machines, I listen to the purrs and beeps

while I await the radiologist's verdict.
I am not afraid exactly; I am chilled with a cold
that constricts in the unknown. I play with what it
might feel like to hear bad news - like wading

through mud or holding my breath to the point
of gasping, like reaching the shock point
in a horror movie when the victim drops
her keys just as the masked killer lunges.

The woman in the next cubicle is taken
to ultrasound. Her gown crackles as she walks.
Through the slit in the curtain, our eyes meet,
two prisoners facing the same harsh judge.

The machine hums a low tune, then high notes
of warning. The cold moves like a living shade
when the nurse calls my name. She writes my future
on the chart before she hands me my clothes.

These Words Are for You

You stand at the edge –
Sooner or later, you must
Drop your fear of heights.

Part Two

Absence

the vast night—
now nothing left
but the fragrance

-Jorge Luis Borge

The "Not" Poem

This is not how things should be, holed up in a motel room,
not pretty or comfortable, not even clean. Just when
our mother tells us we are not waiting for you anymore,
you arrive, and we watch her straddle relief and anger.

Things feel not far from right but not far from wrong either.
Our mother does not ask where you have been and you do not
tell her. You say - *If that is not the roar of the ocean I hear
in this beat-up motel, I don't know what it is* – except you

do not say beat-up motel, you do not say this place not on the strip,
not near the arcade and the pizza kitchen, the one you do not like.
You do not say you will drive us those few blocks to the public beach.
You do not offer to gather us in your arms and carry us over

hot sand to the line where the aqua water turns it cool gray.
We will not go without you, my mother's firm mouth now says.
She does not look at you. We do not know what to do except to not
look at you either. We wonder when we will not have to do this

anymore.

The Taxi

The back seat.

The dark interior of the cab.

The dark street, wet with rain.

The boy in wet clothes, looking out the back window.

Looking at what he's leaving.

Looking at what he might not see again.

The police lights flashing the scene.

The sick struggle of a woman.

The woman who left her child by himself all day.

The woman who loves her child.

The woman who loves a drink.

The boy who doesn't cry.

The boy who's seen a river of tears.

The river of rainwater in the drainage ditch.

The lights of the police, blue like water.

The woman in a dress, blue like police lights.

The boy with wide eyes, hands pressed against the window.

The taxi speeding away.

Tintern Abbey Revisited

Standing in this shell of cathedral,
walls stony silent, ceiling sky-open, wide
as prayers on the lips of monks centuries ago,
I see the imprint of holy light through the gaps
in the rose windows, delicate panes of bone
through which the flesh of sun revolves.

Like Wordsworth, who wrote his lines
a few miles above the wooded Wye valley,
I imagine the footsteps of Cistercians,
their low smoldering chant that sounds
more sorrowful than the wind swooping low
to kiss the dark skeleton altar of their worship.

The great hall, adorned by absence of stained glass
and abandoned earthly praise, has four walls
which lift like arms to call God back, to sound
the truth of its great past, when men in blue robes
of discipline and penitence, walked the aisles
between the wine, the bread, the anointing oil.

My breath rises in the weighted chill of morning,
puddles crust at the icy edge, and weeds
brush like folded prayer-books at the corners
of my heart, where unremembered devotion
still wanders somewhere between intellect
and innocence, that place the soul never abandons.

Tintern Abbey, in its silence, calls me
to the holiness in the jeweled sky, while doves
offer hymns in voices untrained, unpolished,
the chant lifting past panes that once held
Christ Risen in colored light, and now holds
at its center, a thousand year old cross of stone.

The Whistle Blower

> *In the war in Congo, young children are used as bait to draw out the enemy and receive the first round of bullets. The only thing they carry is a whistle.*

Too small to hold a gun,
too weak to fight, still
a purpose for me in this
dark Congo – a whistle
I hold in my teeth,
my breath deep and young,
every exhale the song
of the siren, high, bright,
shrill against the rain
that mutes the earth.

Hear me, I come.

Yanked from my bed
in the safe cradle
of my village, stolen,
my mother's voice
in torment before
the bullet made silence.
I hold in my teeth
a whistle, a trill,
a shriek, the sound
I cry in my dreams.

Hear me, I come.

Behind me are the men
who pull the trigger
so I will not run. In front
are the men who pull
the trigger so I cannot run.
I am the shield of flesh
between them, my metal
voice screaming before
the slash and slay of
the Congo's brutal heart.

Hear me, I come.

The Lawyer's Office

She sits in a lawyer's office
her purse in her lap

dark mahogany, plush fabrics, city view

She worries about her son
how she will let go of this dream

family, home, security, love

She knows her face has the sunken
gray appearance of someone ill

revulsion, nightmare, betrayal, loss

She tries to remember the time line
how the clues fell into chilling fact

suspicion, disbelief, anger, pain

She tries to forget his face
as it twisted into a stranger's

lies, excuses, deception, farce

She imagines how it will feel
for her son to have two homes

confusion, disillusionment, grief

She hovers over the document
that will change everything

exhaustion, numbness, signature, date

Bus 64

Notorious for thieves, Bus 64 travels Corso Vittorio Emmanule
from the Roman historic center to the Vatican. Travelers bump,
hug their bags closer, try not to be what they are – tourists
capturing memories, photographs, on this rainy Rome morning.

We watch them like spies from our seat in the back,
as they study public transit maps and check for passports
tucked in fabric security pockets. I used to check too, before
I forgot who I am and no amount of checking secured the truth.

I used to watch for the pickpockets, hands deep in the fabric
of their coats until, with a flash, they sliced open the bottom
of some woman's purse. I wondered how she could not tell
the sudden lightness, the drain of all she is. Not anymore.

People don't notice, don't value their soul until it's gone,
until it travels on Bus 64 away from them and they are standing
at the Vatican without their camera, without their maps, without
any way to get back to themselves. You bump my arm

and we edge out, stand silent as crowds pass, both of us wrapped
inside the living remnant of what we thought so indispensable.
We walk, our hands hidden in coat pockets that could hide
anything, and neither of us knows who is victim, who is thief.

Family Cemetery

Down the long row of markers my mind rambles,
reciting names matched to faces of long ago. Dirt is piled,
covered by a tarp and laced down with ties.
What is open now is more than grief.

To look into a grave is like looking into both the future
and the past - the prospect of living with loss, remembrances
of a time gone by and over. The body is a haven
for the soul for such a brief season.

There is an art to burial, the gravediggers say –
precision and symmetry, exact measurements and right angles,
the centered headstone and etched dates.
Even grief is lovely in its meticulous pain.

The preacher says this is not an end, but a beginning.
Somewhere in death is life; somewhere in pain is joy. I wonder,
as the dirt is mounded, the flowers bold, proud,
the prayers lifting

to a God who claims his own, why my heart
feels so strange, its beat tenuous and uncertain, as if
it can't quite believe in the everlasting
amid this scrupulous finality.

My Father's Lament

The tops of trees are bare, jutting toward the blank soul of sky.

It won't be long before yellow leaves in the tree's center drop,
and then the bottom will fade like a hollowed-out thought
when the meaning no longer has passion.

I know the trees will fill again, that this slight death is temporary,
but the crackle of dry leaves under my feet reminds me of bones.

A tree's skeleton is trunk, branch, a beautiful burl and grain
renewed as something useful and lasting.

How will I be reborn, but as a breeze, a whisper.

I wish I had set my heart deep like roots, past the brief victories
stacked between ordinary moments. I hardly remember them now.

One white light against another. One frozen sky.

Already, the brush of winter takes my breath. The color of my bones
stretch into what's left and find nothing I can call summer,
no fragrant lake, no deep rush of heat beneath a moaning sky,

no yearning stars, no golden glaze on the back of dragonflies,
no secret promises beneath the pine.

Already, I am falling, bare hands reaching upward, and already,
I have no memory of the blue.

Burn After Reading

If I told you my secrets, perhaps the moon itself
would blaze with the reality of fire.

If I said, for instance, I stole my grandfather's lighter
and with the boy next door, burned a library book
in a ring of dirt, would you think I was a pyromaniac?

If I told you I sat by a tent and watched a boyfriend sniff
the fumes of Dove Flexible Hold before spraying it

in a campfire, whooshing white flame, if I said
we emptied the powder from firecrackers and burned
the word *hell* into the sidewalk by our school,

would you think I wanted power? Maybe I only wanted
light and warmth, maybe a link with someone outside

the wide blank rooms of my home. Maybe I needed to see
clearly, to feel the retinas in my eyes sting with something
that mattered more than beer and sex and cigarettes.

If I told you my fingers could be candles, my feet rockets
holding solid fuel, enough to lift me far from town,

catching sun flares in my arms to kindle dreams,
that would be too much. So I'll tell you
the fire in the dry grass behind the convenience store

began as a flicker of hope, flint against steel,
a spark flaring into a conflagration, wide and wild,

lighting the sky and spreading like orange flood
through the thin shrubs and scrubby thoughts,
as the sirens cut secrets out of the darkness.

Quiet Me
for P. and M.

Quiet me with your eyes
the way you used to when early mornings
sang the earth awake and you would
slide your coat over your shoulders,
your arms through in one easy shrug -
like a dancer or an acrobat -
the same way she twisted and curved
in those floaty dreams. Remember
how she said she could drift when the pain
became too much and the little pill
on her tongue, bitter as chalk,
promised sleep. At least that's what we
told her, *it will help you sleep* - how
we wanted to believe it.
You wanted to put on your coat,
shimmy it on like a caress, and walk
through the dewy grass stirring
the mist. In those mornings
I heard you and set the dizzy rattle
of my blood a moment steady,
your eyes widened so blue,
so clear, I thought the sky
could never compete, and you said
nothing, but your eyes said *secret*,
and *silence*, and *promise*, and I knew
in all the world there was no kinder way
to tell me how you ached
to see your little girl dying, how
sometimes it was so raw you needed
something cold and bone-jarring
to mute it - you with your coat
and the acrid morning, the dew
on the tall grass, your breath rising
in little prayers, your boots marking time
for the quiet mornings
that pierce us now.

Naming Bones

Put me in the ground before I get like that, my mother whispered,
aghast as we stood beside the bed of her friend. Tubes coiled
from the wasted chest; the girth of diaper bunched beneath the gown.

When he was five, my son insisted on burying the red wasp
I killed in the kitchen. He carried the body solemnly on a napkin
and dug the grave with a spoon. *Ashes to ashes*, he prayed,

dust to dust in crumbling Haiti as a father rescued his son's body
from the mass graves, poured Quikrete on the bare ground,
and with his fingers, mixed it with water, mounded it to stone.

He must be named, the father explained, his face tolling loss.
What was the wasp's name? asked my son as he carried the spoon.
She hardly knows her name, my mother frowned, shaking her head.

What do we call these bones reaped by death's iron scythe?
How do we reconcile their innocence? In Haiti, a dead boy waits
while his father carves his name in concrete with a stick.

The River
for Samuel

The river rides high tonight, four days
of rain filling the hollows, spreading
the spongy sod until it is full – too full –
and what it cannot hold runs wild.

The murky brown-black of a living soul,
the gravid voice that is labored, shrill -
what do we know of a river's dreams
to escape its tall walls and wander?

And what did we know of your dreams,
how it was to be young, to want
so much beyond what you could reach,
what did we know of the strength

of the current within your veins?
You and the river are one tonight,
both of you swollen and raw, a naked
gash against the earth and still wanting.

The land seeps out of your eyes, dark
wanting on the bank where the river
spit you out, all the sorrow and suffering,
all the high dead words spilling

out of your eyes, the voiceless speech
of dreams surging, spreading your heart
until it is full – too full.
And what it cannot hold runs wild.

Love Like This

    for Clay

When they told you the pain would fade,
        you nodded your face smeared red with grief,
but in your heart, you knew they lied.

You knew you would carry pain like this
        all your days, and you wanted to, because
even in your short ten years of life,

you knew love carried within its bright buoyancy
        the capacity for jagged pain.
The price of love was pain like this,

and you wouldn't trade it for anything
        because it meant a love like this birthed it,
balanced it. You knew, even as you placed

your quivering mouth on his
        and tried to spread his lungs with air.
You knew, even as you held your face

against his sunken chest
        and sobbed at how hard you tried but you couldn't
bring him back. You knew.

Pain like this was necessary
        for love like this. When you stood at his coffin
and placed your small hands

on his cold ones, you knew the adults stared.
        And when you repeated out loud "He's gone,"
you knew it was for them as much as for you.

They had to hear it,
        for pain like this must be spoken. Even though
the words rising from your clear high voice

sounded wretched, you said it again and again,
        your ten years of life bending the stillness
of such a deep truth until the room was loud with it,

pain like this, love like this.

My 1963

January third, four days late. My disappointed father -
he's forced to wait a year for the deduction.

My mother settles into darkness having two girls in two years.
A blue bow taped to my temple.

The color of boys but it matches a blue blanket. My mother
and I cry together. My sister holds me, calls me baby.

I am no one's baby.
Alone on a hand-me-down quilt, the shadows of trees.

From my mother I learn the language of tears, silver letters.
A thin baby. I grow anyway, can't help myself.

Watching my mother's face I learn you must
hold on to something.

There is violence in the world, even against Presidents.
A song breaks into small syllables and ends.

Dressed in blue except at Christmas – red, to match my sister.
Wispy hair and the ribbon dangles like an ornament.

A new winter, a new start. Learning to crawl,
I learn to escape.

My mother's belly swollen with another girl. Those four days
might have changed everything.

How It Started

Before he sat on asphalt with a blue blanket over his shoulders,
images spinning through his mind like a film strip,

Before he wiped river water from his eyes and shook his head
at how quickly hell had reared up to swallow him,

Before hell barely missed and he caught a rope and hung on,
and a man who might have been Jesus pulled him
into a motorboat,

Before he trembled in the water, choking down panic,
his arms and legs so heavy they felt like tree limbs,

Before he yelled to Roy to just hold on a little longer, and Roy
slipped beneath the gray water, sucked down like a dog,

Before he realized the boat he and Roy fought so frantically to control
would not withstand the crushing force of the water,

Before the sluice gates were opened and the current became
a monster that whipped the boat like a bathtub toy,

Before he began to have serious doubts about the worthiness
of Roy's boat, and Roy laughed at him and said what the hell,
it's as good as any other,

Before Roy called him around noon and asked if he wanted
to go fishing below Center Hill dam, and he said yeah, all right,
mostly to spite Miranda,

Before he was more than a little pissed at Miranda for nagging him
about the toilet that needed to be fixed even when she knew
how hard he worked,

Before he turned on the TV just to see what was on, and settled
back on the couch as if he'd be parked there all day,

He woke on Saturday morning and saw, after a week of rain,
the sun finally out, rays filtering through the last of the clouds,
luminous and strangely beautiful.

Sister

for Kelly

There is still the apology I owe,
thirty-five years heavy.

I ponder how to say it, how
to apologize for being older,

making the rules, expecting
you to follow my direction,

and when, at the dangerous
age of thirteen, I decided

I didn't need a little sister,
using my superior wisdom

to ignore you, deride your
attempts to play like we

used to, like girls instead of
budding women. It wasn't

that I wanted to leave you
and the maple tree we scaled

like monkeys, the old hideout
in the barn, the square of asphalt

we primed as a kickball field
with trashcan lids for bases.

Things were expected, you
understand. I had to run

from you and not look back
at our childhood, safe

and simple, soft in the tent
we made under the sky

of a thousand wishes,
under a love that, afterwards,

was never quite the same.

The Cardinal

for P.

    For three mornings since the funeral, you watch a cardinal
fling himself into the kitchen window. Despite what you do to deter him,
he launches from the dogwood branch to crush his beak and wings
on reflected blue. You see him sink and rise again, startled and confused,
cocking his head to consider what might be required to break this band of air.

    You jump at every thud, and the morning strains
with this useless beating, this resistance against unflinching authority.
Every blow becomes a club against your back, a far-flung pain circled
round to bend into you again. It becomes as heavy as a bucket filled
with red clay, as your father's casket in the hard-baked earth.

    You press your hands against the glass, and then
your face, but you cannot hold that pose. As soon as you leave, the bird
resumes his reckless riot, his eye sealed to the boiling sun, resolute
to his own destruction. You ask yourself if you can bear it and the answer
comes with anger - the bitter taste of grief and abandoned promises.

    You stand at the window and stare. The cardinal,
desperate for his cage, will not turn to take the clear and breathless sky.
The song of his breaking recoils like an echo. You ask yourself if you
can accept it and the answer comes with sorrow – your father's face,
the pardon you wanted to give him and never did.

Old Growth Forest
for my father

Baxter Cabin stands a hundred years down the Maddron Bald Trail,
chestnut boards and stone chimney mark a shadow against streaming light.
I have learned not to ask questions about the past when we hike -
you, a sturdy wedge of bone and bitterness, and me, hopeful daughter,
eager, even in this silence.

I listen to the trudge of your boots, your deep baritone swearing
at missteps – at the slight gully where the rainwater washed the dirt
from under a fallen branch, or the ooze of slimy mold on the flat plane
of a rock. The words sound like metal in this hollow of ecology,
like bolts dropping in a bowl.

The trail slopes upward, rising on the ridge above Indian Camp Creek,
but we break south toward Albright Grove and the old-growth hardwoods
you pledged to see. Basswood breathes through heart-large leaves,
lifted like offerings to the sun, while beech and magnolia flirt
beneath the cave-dark canopy.

We've come for the tuliptree, the one that tops a hundred feet
and claims the outstretched arms of five people to circle it. A narrow
spur trail leads us there, and I look up to see the blue beyond
the dense woody green. You watch as I count how many times
I can curve my reed-thin arms around,

pressing my chest and then my back against the furrowed bark
to keep my place along its girth. In the deep hush, I hear your footsteps
rooting the path again. I see the shape of your shoulders hunched
beneath your coat, the layered browns meshing together as you leave.
It's stillness that tires you;

the sudden shudder of an binding grief. Frasers and hemlocks,
spared by loggers and unshaken by blight, bow like monks before
the vesper altar. Though your absence is familiar, I can never quite
silence despair. Following you, as I have done for as long as I remember,
I circle back to the Bald,

walking the last miles alone. I know I will find you, your grim mouth
glued shut, your fingers flipping through the trail guide, adding another
mark to the list of trails completed, those we hike together alone,
both of us on the same different path to get where you are going,
to get you back somehow.

The Sugar Maple Speaks

They say the oldest trees in this neighborhood
are beginning to die. For three hundred years,
I've spread wings under this earth, beyond clay
and the sharp shelves of limestone. I've reached
halfway to the sun, laid canopies over grass.
No year turns forgotten in the rings of my spirit.

I've seen Cherokee drum the moon down,
and calicoed ladies swing to violins. I've seen
soldiers lift muskets of despair and fire into bone.
I've heard train whistles and school bus horns,
and breathed the poisoned gas of factories.
I've endured tornadoes, and defied cracked lightning.

I've weathered thrips and borers, the needle-sting
of woodpecker's syringe, and the gypsy moth's
sticky swell. I remember wing-wild seeds, and stories
within the wind's breath, and every secret pressed
against my skin, and every wish tossed high.
I've been a trapeze worn smooth by fingers of children

and have held the backs of men. I've witnessed rage
and glee, and pitied the spasmodic lurch of those who
struggle to be still, who chase their hearts and seethe.
I am lucky. I am friends with nymphs and fairies.
I've watched the airy ritual of mockingbirds and the squirrel's
carnival. I've been fed by clouds and lingered in sleep.

I return to dawn as every prayer returns to itself.
Death leads back to birth in the calm of my sap's
un-rising: tree to tree, sapling to seedling, sprout
to winged seed floating from the eaves of my aged heart.
There is no reason for regret. It's in a tree's nature
to be grateful. And I am. So be it. Amen.

Poem for a Cat

I don't know your name, or even if you have one,
but I will ask you politely not to kill the baby birds
that fall from their woven nests or the rabbits
sunning unguarded amidst the rogue dandelions
in my manicured yard. I will ask you, slinky rover,
not to slip into my garage like a vandal, and paint
graffiti on my windshield with your fancy dust paws,
leaving the remnant of your musty pheromone.

I concede to you the wooded lot behind the fence,
the mice and snakes, all the grasshoppers you can spear
with your needle claws. I give you the creek rushes,
the sweet heather and catmint growing wild
by the rocky path. You, with your marble green
eyes slit with gold, your cashmere coat gray as a mink,
do me this favor. And I, in return, will be your confidant,
the one you sing to in your hoarse accent on the coldest
wettest nights, even though when I call to you,
you do not trust me enough to come.

Notes

"On Waiting for a Tow Truck in a Church Parking Lot" – Forest Hills Baptist Church – Nashville, TN – Thanks for the reminder.

"A Ninety-Seven-Year-Old Speaks of Death" – recalling a conversation with my great grandmother, Mary Huldah Garrett Peters (August 30, 1895 – March 13, 1993).

"Murmurs" – after watching "Gretna Green Starling Murmurations" by wildaboutimages, video published on Nov 21, 2013.

"When You Write" – after reading "These Days" by Charles Olson – "Whatever you have to say, leave the roots on, let them dangle . . ."

"Tintern Abbey Revisited" – after standing in the ruins of Tintern Abbey, Gwent County, Wales - July 2011.

"Family Cemetery" – Piedmont Cemetery, Jefferson County, TN.

"The River" – the line "the land seeps out of (Darl's) eyes" is from *As I Lay Dying* by William Faulkner.

"Love Like This" – after the death of Kenneth Leslie Spencer (April 2, 1939 – March 10, 2013) - Rest in peace, Uncle.

"My 1963" – after reading *My Life* by Lyn Hejinian.

About the Author

Sandy Coomer's poetry chapbook, *Continuum*, was published by Finishing Line Press in 2012. *The Presence of Absence* is her second collection. She is active in her community's poetry critique groups and open mic's, and is a reader for "Poets from the Neighborhood," a public access television segment featuring and promoting the works of local poets. A mixed media and watercolor artist, she enjoys creating whimsical and uplifting art pieces that blend objects and words together in themes of family, home, and belief in self. An avid endurance athlete, she regularly competes in marathons, ultra marathons, and triathlons, including the inaugural full distance Ironman Chattanooga Triathlon in September 2014. She lives in Brentwood, TN with her husband and four children.

www.ingramcontent.com/pod-product-compliance
Lightning Source LLC
Chambersburg PA
CBHW031430290426
44110CB00011B/598